discovermore
Earth Science

The Water Cycle

Theia Lake

Britannica
Educational Publishing
IN ASSOCIATION WITH
THE ROSEN PUBLISHING GROUP

Published in 2026 by Britannica Educational Publishing (a trademark of Encyclopædia Britannica, Inc.) in association with The Rosen Publishing Group, Inc.
2544 Clinton Street, Buffalo, NY 14224

Distributed exclusively by Rosen Publishing.
To see additional Britannica Educational Publishing titles, go to rosenpublishing.com.

Editor: Danielle Haynes
Book Design: Michael Flynn

Photo Credits: Cover Nick Fox/Shutterstock.com; (series background) Dai Yim/Shutterstock.com; p. 4 March Studio/Shutterstock.com; p. 5 MNStudio/Shutterstock.com; p. 6 Blueastro/Shutterstock.com; p. 7 muratart/Shutterstock.com; p. 8 Viktoria Kytt/Shutterstock.com; p. 9 Vasilisa_Musina2/Shutterstock.com; p. 10 laponpat maliwan/Shutterstock.com; p. 11 Barbol/Shutterstock.com; p. 12 Russ Heinl/Shutterstock.com; p. 13 pixfly/Shutterstock.com; p. 14 Ana del Castillo/Shutterstock.com; p. 15 Jonah Lange/Shutterstock.com; p. 16 Nattapol_Sritongcom/Shutterstock.com; p. 17 Saint Images/Shutterstock.com; p. 18 Matt Ivanov/Shutterstock.com; p. 19 Janelle Lugge/Shutterstock.com; p. 20 TayHamPhotography/Shutterstock.com; p. 21 chaossart/Shutterstock.com; p. 22 Flystock/Shutterstock.com; p. 23 Denys.Kutsevalov/Shutterstock.com; p. 24 zombiu26/Shutterstock.com; p. 25 Sonia Bonet/Shutterstock.com; p. 26 GreenOak/Shutterstock.com; p. 27 Lost_in_the_Midwest/Shutterstock.com; p. 28 Prostock-studio/Shutterstock.com; p. 29 Olya Detry/Shutterstock.com.

Cataloging-in-Publication Data

Names: Lake, Theia.
Title: The water cycle / Theia Lake.
Description: New York : Britannica Educational Publishing, in association with Rosen Educational Services, 2026. | Series: Discover more: earth science | Includes glossary and index.
Identifiers: ISBN 9781641904315 (library bound) | ISBN 9781641904308 (pbk) | ISBN 9781641904322 (ebook)
Subjects: LCSH: Hydrologic cycle--Juvenile literature.
Classification: LCC GB848.L35 2026 | DDC 551.48--dc23

Manufactured in the United States of America

Contents

Water, Water Everywhere 4
The Water Cycle 6
Evaporation 8
Evaporating Plants 10
Condensation 12
Cloudy Skies 14
Rain and Mountains 16
Frozen Precipitation 18
Collecting Underground 20
Moving Through the Cycle 22
Clean Water 24
Pollution 26
Water Conservation 28
Glossary 30
For More Information 31
Index 32

Water, Water Everywhere

Water is everywhere—in us and around us. There is water in rivers, lakes, and oceans. There is also water in the air and in the ground. There is water inside plants and inside animals, too, including people!

About 71 percent of the Earth's surface is covered in water.

Water brings important nutrients to our cells, helps get rid of waste in the body, and keeps our body temperature steady.

Most of Earth's water is in the oceans. Ocean water contains salt. Water in rivers, lakes, and ponds is called fresh water, because it does not contain salt.

Water makes up more than half of our body weight, but we lose some water every day. We drink liquid to replace the water that we lose. Humans can last for weeks without food but would die within days without water. Some animals have adapted to last months and even years without water!

Consider This

Can you list the ways that people use water each day?

The Water Cycle

Water is always on the move. It is constantly recycled. Recycling means to take something old and change it into something new. Earth's water is continually moving from one place to another and from one form to another. Water leaves Earth's surface and rises into the air. Later, gravity pulls it back to Earth in the form of rain or snow. This process is called the water cycle.

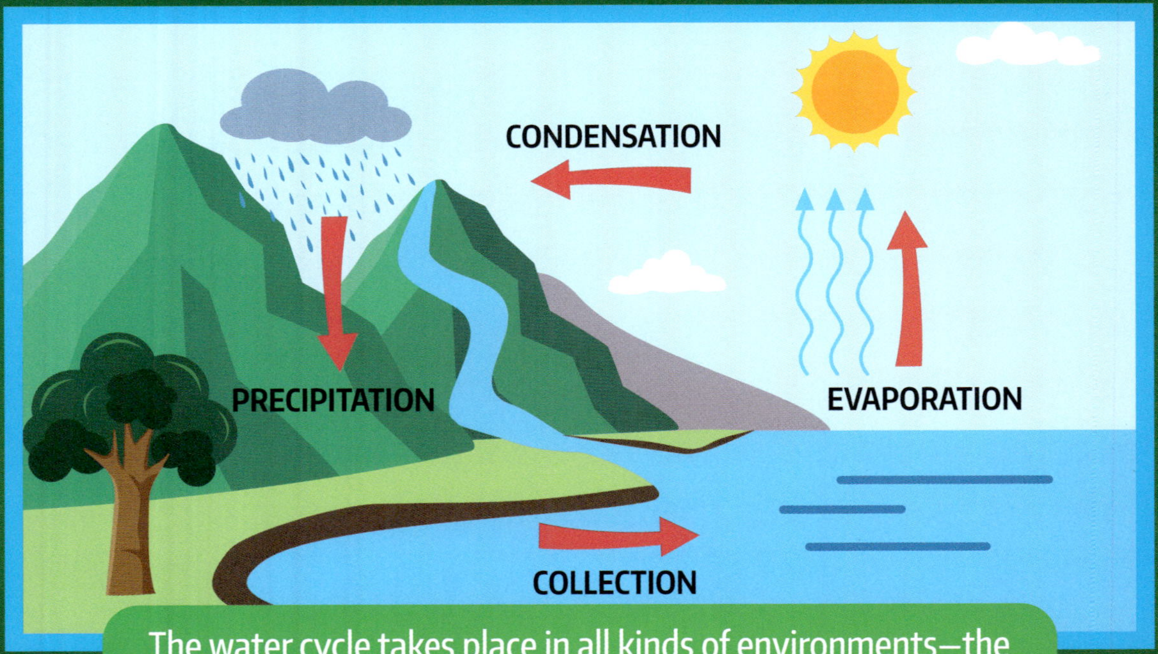

The water cycle takes place in all kinds of environments—the oceans, the mountains, even the deserts!

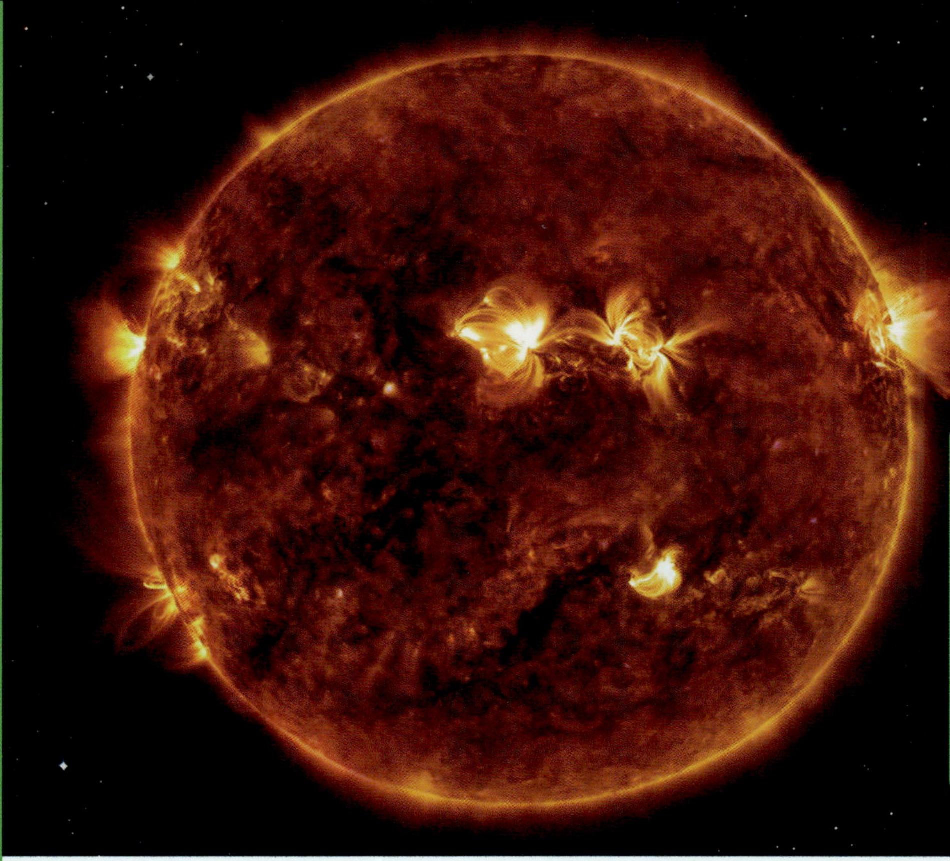

Solar activity includes things such as sunspots and prominences, which are large, bright features extending out from the surface of the sun.

Things need **energy** to make them work. It is heat from the sun that provides the energy to make the water cycle work. Although the sun is far from Earth, its surface is so hot that some of its heat travels through space to Earth. The sun gives off huge amounts of heat energy. Changes in the solar activity can impact the water cycle.

WORD WISE

ENERGY IS POWER THAT CAN MAKE THINGS WORK, MOVE, LIVE, AND GROW.

Evaporation

Some scientists believe the sun is the single most important part of the water cycle because it fuels evaporation. When the sun shines, it heats up water at the surface of rivers, lakes, and oceans. At a certain temperature, this water evaporates. This means that it changes from a liquid to a gas. As a gas it floats in the air. A gas is a substance that is usually colorless and invisible and has no shape or size of its own. When water becomes a gas, we call it water vapor.

Here you can see water evaporating as it heats up in a pot on the stove.

Only fresh water evaporates from the ocean, leaving behind the salt. Some of this evaporated fresh water then goes on to rain down on land, helping plants grow.

We see evaporation in action every day. We see it when we hang out wet laundry so it can dry in the air. We also see water evaporate quickly as steam when we boil water in a teapot or heat a pan of water. Many times, we don't see it since water vapor can be invisible to the eye. Even the moisture in your skin can evaporate on a dry day.

Consider This

When water evaporates, it takes some heat with it. How does this explain how sweating helps us to cool down on hot days?

Evaporating Plants

A lot of the water evaporated into the atmosphere comes from plants. Plants take in water and nutrients from the ground through their roots to make food and to hold themselves upright. The water and nutrients travel up a plant through little tubes. When water escapes from leaves at the top of the tubes, more water is sucked into the roots.

Rainforests soak up a lot of rainwater but also evaporate quite a bit of water into the atmosphere.

Stomata, the holes through which plants evaporate water, can only be seen under a microscope.

Water escapes from leaves because it evaporates. When the sun warms the leaves, it heats up water inside the leaves, too. This makes some of the water evaporate. It turns into water vapor and passes out of tiny holes in the leaves into the air around them. These tiny holes are called stomata.

Consider This

How is the way water rises up the tubes inside a plant similar to the way we drink through a straw?

Condensation

So what happens with all that water in the air? Condensation. This happens when a gas changes into a liquid. Water vapor is very light, so it floats up into the air. The farther above Earth's surface something travels, the cooler it becomes. As water vapor rises higher in the air, it gets cooler. When water vapor gets cold, it condenses. It changes back into tiny droplets of liquid water. Large groups of these droplets are called clouds.

Vapor trails left by airplanes are also called contrails.

The cold drink on the inside of this glass causes water vapor to condense and form water droplets on the outside of the glass.

We see condensation every day. In a hot bathroom, water vapor from the steamy air condenses into liquid on a cold mirror. When you pour a glass of cold water on a hot day, water forms on the outside of the glass. This is because the water vapor in the warm air turns back into liquid when it touches cold glass. The temperature at which water vapor condenses back into liquid is called the dew point.

Consider This

Why might the windows of a car steam up when there are several people inside it?

Cloudy Skies

When water vapor condenses into tiny drops of water, the drops form clouds. Clouds look light and fluffy, but each one is made up of billions of droplets of water. Clouds move with the wind. Many clouds start to form above oceans, where most water evaporates. Wind blows the vapor over land, where we see clouds gathering.

Big, fluffy clouds such as these are called cumulus clouds. These clouds don't typically produce precipitation.

Cumulonimbus clouds are likely to produce thunderstorms. They're tall with flat bottoms and often have a dark wall of clouds hanging beneath.

There are different types of clouds. The type of cloud depends on how much water vapor it contains, how cold the air is in the sky where it is, and what the wind is doing. If wind blows a cloud into warm air, the droplets of water that make up the cloud evaporate, and the cloud disappears. If it is cooler, more and more water vapor condenses in the air. Then clouds grow bigger and darker. The big, dark clouds that produce thunderstorms are known as cumulonimbus clouds.

Consider This

Why do you think just one small cloud weighs as much as 100 elephants?

Rain and Mountains

Water vapor doesn't just stay in the atmosphere forever. Droplets of water spend about eight days in the sky. They are blown about by the wind. As the droplets of water that make up a cloud blow about, they bump into each other and form bigger and bigger drops of water. When the drops of water become too big and heavy to float, they fall from the sky as rain.

Rain is an important part of the water cycle because it provides fresh water to plants and animals that need it to survive.

The landscape on one side of a mountain can look dramatically different from the other side thanks to the rain shadow.

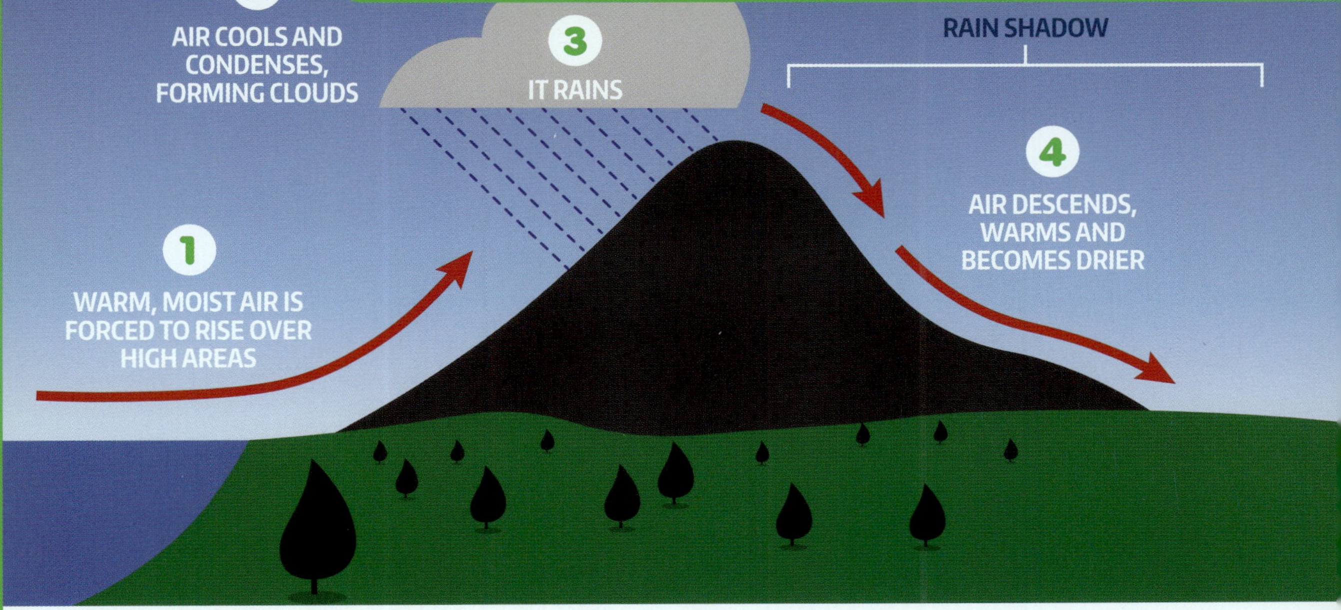

As wind blows clouds across land, some clouds meet high areas of land called mountains. The steep sides of a mountain force clouds higher up into the sky. This cools more water vapor in the clouds, which falls to the ground as rain. The air is so cold that high up in the sky that raindrops often start out as snowflakes before melting as they fall.

Consider This

A rain shadow is a patch of land on one side of a mountain that is very dry. How might the water cycle cause this?

Frozen Precipitation

Sometimes, snowflakes don't melt as they fall from the clouds. If it's cold enough on the ground or if the clouds go high enough into the atmosphere, precipitation happens in the form of snow and ice. Some clouds rise up quickly through the sky to the point where the air is very, very cold. There, water droplets freeze. They change from water to solid ice. The ice may fall to Earth as hailstones, which are small balls of ice, or it may fall as snowflakes. After snow and ice hit the ground, they eventually melt into water once more.

Snowflakes may look like little white blobs, but take a closer look to see their crystalline structure.

On average, the ice at the South Pole is 1.5 miles (2.4 km) thick. It's nearly 3 miles (4.8 km) thick in some spots!

In the coldest parts of the world, snow never melts. Instead, new layers of snow build up on old layers of snow. The weight of the upper layers eventually turns the lower layers to ice. In fact, about 70 percent of all the fresh water in the world is frozen into ice at the North and South Poles. These areas are also known as the polar ice caps.

Consider This

Earth is getting warmer, and ice at the poles is melting. What will happen to the ice then?

Collecting Underground

Not all the water that falls to Earth stays on land. Some of it runs into rivers or seeps into soil. Some sinks through cracks in the rock below soil to go deep underground. This groundwater collects in holes in underground rock or forms underground pools or streams. Groundwater sources store huge amounts of fresh water.

Water collects underground in the caves of Okinawa, Japan.

People in Austria built a fountain to bring spring water out for people to use.

Some groundwater rises to Earth's surface through natural openings called springs. People also drill holes called wells into land to reach groundwater. Some groundwater is pumped to the surface by machines. More than half the people in the United States get their drinking water from groundwater supplies.

Consider This

What happens to groundwater when waste from dumps and gas from petroleum seep underground?

Moving Through the Cycle

Whether fast or slow, water is always moving in the water cycle. Sometimes, it moves quickly. For example, rain evaporates off a surface, such as a puddle on a sidewalk, almost at once. Some water moves more slowly through the cycle. Ice can stay frozen in a glacier for thousands of years before it melts and flows into a lake. It can then stay in the lake for thousands of years before evaporating into the air again.

Puddles on a hot day won't stick around for long. They'll evaporate quickly.

Ice that has been frozen as part of a glacier for thousands of years may suddenly break apart and fall into the ocean. That ice will slowly melt into the warmer ocean water.

Water may stay under the ground for thousands of years. Gradually it may be taken up by plant roots and returned to the air through leaves. Water may also soak into streams, which flow into a river. Rivers flow into oceans, so some groundwater will evaporate from the ocean. Water has been on Earth for billions of years. Think of all the places each drop has been!

Consider This

What do you think happens to rain that falls on land or snow that melts to water?

Clean Water

In many ways, the water cycle is a self-cleaning process. Water goes on and on flowing, evaporating, condensing, and falling back to Earth, where it flows again. The water cycle has been happening for billions of years. The water cycle means we can use the same water again and again and again!

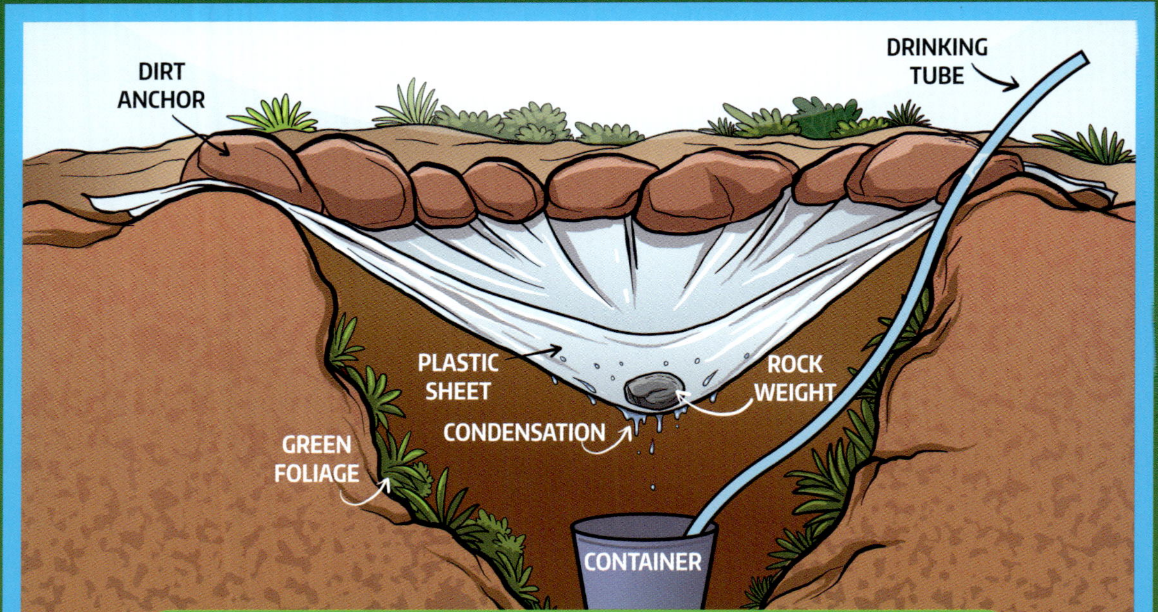

Survivalists can make their own device called a solar water still to clean dirty groundwater. This uses a sheet of plastic to condense and collect evaporated water.

Humans have been using solar evaporation to extract salt from seawater for hundreds of years.

The water cycle also cleans the water that evaporates from Earth. As water evaporates and changes from a liquid into a gas, any dirt that was in it is lost. The water in the oceans is salty, and we cannot drink or use it. However, when it evaporates, the salt is left behind. The water is now clean and falls back to Earth as fresh water we can drink. People have even used evaporation ponds to take salt out of seawater to use in our food.

Consider This

Why could the water we drink today once have been drunk by the dinosaurs?

Pollution

Just because water is cleaned through evaporation doesn't mean all water is safe. Water is cleaned when it goes through the water cycle, but it can be on Earth hundreds or thousands of years before it evaporates. When we **pollute** water on Earth, we reduce the amount of clean water we can use. People pollute water by dumping things in it, such as litter and dirty water from buildings and factories.

Oil spills in the ocean make the water unsafe for sea creatures and plants.

In some places, water that goes into storm drains goes directly into lakes and streams. This is why it's important to clean up pet waste in the grass.

There are many things people can do to help keep the world's water clean. They can avoid throwing paints, oils, and litter down sinks or drains, or into rivers, lakes, and oceans. They can use household cleaners and bathroom products that are not harmful to the environment. They can also always pick up their dog's waste to make sure it doesn't go into storm drains.

WORD WISE

TO POLLUTE IS TO ADD DIRTY OR HARMFUL THINGS TO AIR, SOIL, OR WATER.

Water Conservation

Even though water is constantly moving through the water cycle, it's still important not to waste it. One way to make sure there is enough clean fresh water in the future is to reduce the amount we use today. There are lots of ways to save water. People can save up to 8 gallons (30 L) of water every day by turning off the faucet while they brush their teeth. We can save around 10 gallons (38 L) of water by taking a quick shower instead of a bath.

Turning off the water while you brush your teeth is a great way to save water.

Think about using a rain barrel to collect rainwater. This water may not be safe to drink, but it's useful for watering plants and washing cars.

Families can save water by collecting rain that falls on their house and into gutters. Then they can use it to wash cars and water plants, rather than using water from the faucet. Companies are also making dishwashers and other machines that use less water than they did before. It may seem like there's endless water coming out of our faucets, but cleaning, moving, and storing it takes time, money, and energy. Use this precious resource sparingly!

Consider This

How do you think farmers save water by watering plants in the evening when there is less sunshine?

Glossary

crystalline: Having the appearance of a crystal, clear or sparkling with geometric shapes.

environment: The natural world around us.

faucet: The fixture attached to a pipe where water comes out.

gutter: A trough attached to the roof of buildings to catch rainwater.

invisible: Unable to be seen.

nutrient: Something taken in by a plant or animal that helps it grow and stay healthy.

petroleum: An oily, flammable liquid obtained from the Earth by humans to use as fuel or to create products such as plastic.

precipitation: Water that falls to the ground as hail, mist, rain, sleet, or snow.

solar water still: A device that uses heat from the sun to evaporate dirty groundwater or seawater, then collects the clean water as condensation.

stoma: A small hole on a plant leaf that allows water inside the plant to evaporate.

sunspot: Dark spots that sometimes appear on the sun's surface.

survivalist: A person who is prepared to survive the wilderness or without modern conveniences.

vapor: A substance, such as water, that is in its gaseous state.

For More Information

Books

Andrews, E.C. *Water Pollution.* Buffalo, NY: PowerKids Press, 2024.

Gieseke, Tyler. *The Water Cycle.* Minneapolis, MN: DiscoverRoo, 2023.

Harts, Marie. *The Elements of Weather.* Buffalo, NY: Britannica Educational Publishing, 2025.

Websites

National Geographic Kids: Water Cycle
www.natgeokids.com/uk/discover/science/nature/water-cycle
Read more about the water cycle on the National Geographic Kids website.

SciJinks: Precipitation
www.scijinks.gov/precipitation
Learn all about the different types of precipitation.

Index

A
animals, 4, 5, 16, 26

C
clouds, 12, 14, 15, 16, 17, 18
condensation, 6, 12, 13, 15, 17, 24
conservation, 28, 29

D
deserts, 6

E
energy, 7
evaporation, 6, 8, 9, 10, 11, 15, 22, 23, 24, 25, 26

F
fresh water, 5, 9, 16, 19, 25, 28

G
groundwater, 20, 21, 23, 24

H
human body, 4, 5

L
lakes, 4, 5, 8, 22, 27

M
mountains, 6, 16, 17

O
oceans, 4, 5, 6, 8, 9, 14, 23, 25, 27

P
plants, 4, 9, 10, 11, 16, 23, 26, 29
pollution, 26, 27
precipitation, 6, 9, 14, 15, 16, 17, 18, 19, 20, 22, 23, 24, 29

R
rivers, 4, 5, 8, 20, 23, 27

S
salt water, 5, 25
sun, 7, 8, 11

W
water vapor, 8, 9, 11, 12, 13, 14, 15, 16